Mother Anderson's
SECRET BOOK
WIT & WISDOM

by
Stephen Francis
& Rico

JACANA

Published in 2011 in South Africa by Jacana Media

10 Orange Street, Auckland Park, 2092
PO Box 291784, Melville, 2109
www.jacana.co.za

The moral right of the authors has been asserted.

ISBN 978-1-4314-0107-9

Job no. 001482

Printed and bound by Ultra Litho (Pty) Limited, Johannesburg

See a complete list of Jacana titles at www.jacana.co.za

MOTHER ANDERSON'S SECRET BOOK OF WIT & WISDOM

They say always avoid books on wit and wisdom, because the people who write them don't know what the hell they're talking about.

Except for me. I do know what the hell I'm talking about. And now, I want to share it with you.

You've no doubt heard of the book: *Seven Habits of Highly Effective People?* – Well, I possess eight.

The Power of Now? – I'll teach you not only 'The Power of Now', but *The Power of Just Now* and *The Power of Now-Now*.

The One Minute Manager? – All I need is thirty seconds.

So put yourself in my hands, relax and start reading.

You'll be winning friends, inspiring people, thinking positively, and avoiding the pot-holes on the road less-traveled faster than you can say... *"Eve – it's after five! Where's my gin & tonic?!"*

One seventh of your life is spent
on Monday.

WISDOM TO LIVE BY

1. Always tell the truth. It's the easiest thing to remember.

2. Never use your electrified fence as a clothes line.

3. Always avoid books of wit and wisdom. Most of the people who write them don't know what the hell they're talking about. Except for this one.

4. By the time you make ends meet… they move the ends.

5. Everybody has to believe in something. I believe I'll have another gin and tonic.

6. If you think the sun shines out of your bum, get a better reading light.

A fool and his money should avoid reading emails from Nigeria.

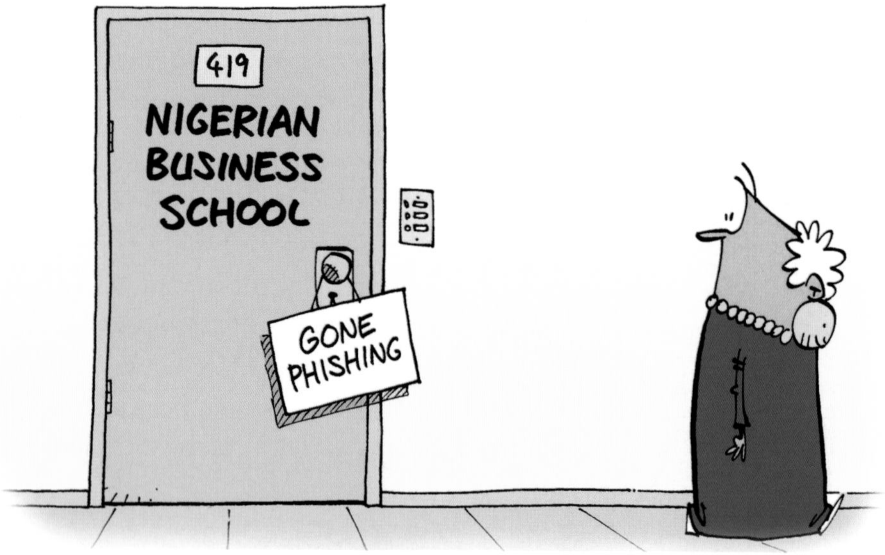
419
NIGERIAN
BUSINESS
SCHOOL
GONE
PHISHING

Those who can… do.
Those who can't… teach.
Those who can, but don't feel like doing…
take long tea breaks.

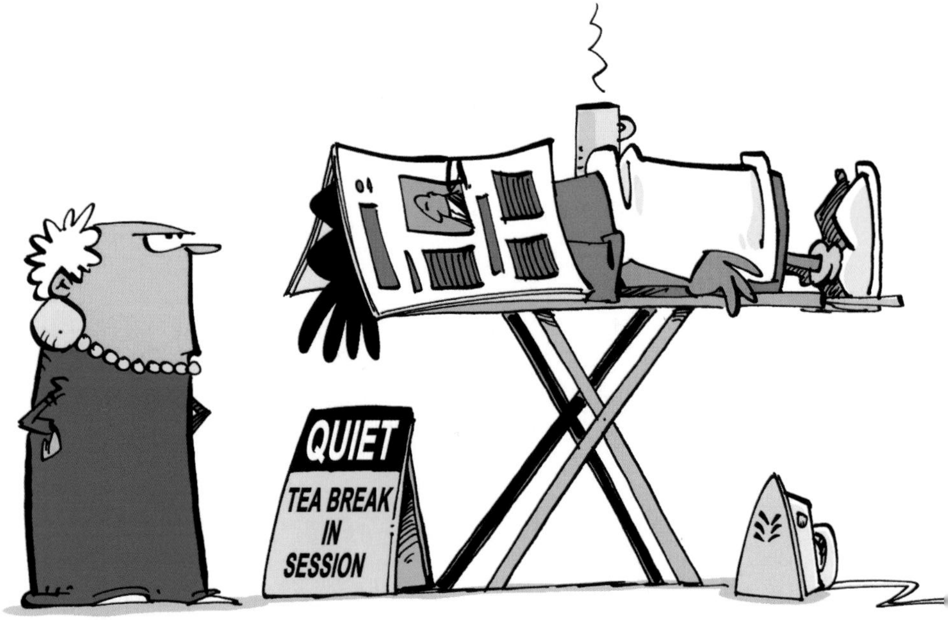
QUIET
TEA BREAK
IN
SESSION

If the grass is always greener on the other side
of the electric fence, fire your gardener and hire
your neighbour's gardener instead.

Never sit unknowingly on a vibrating cell phone.

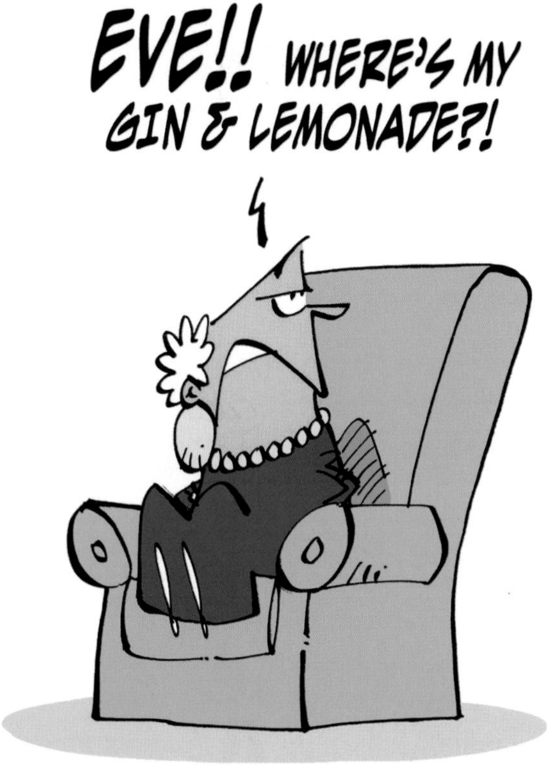
EVE!! WHERE'S MY GIN & LEMONADE?!

If life hands you lemons... ask your maid to make lemonade.

Never hire ADD armed response security.
They can't stay focused on anything.

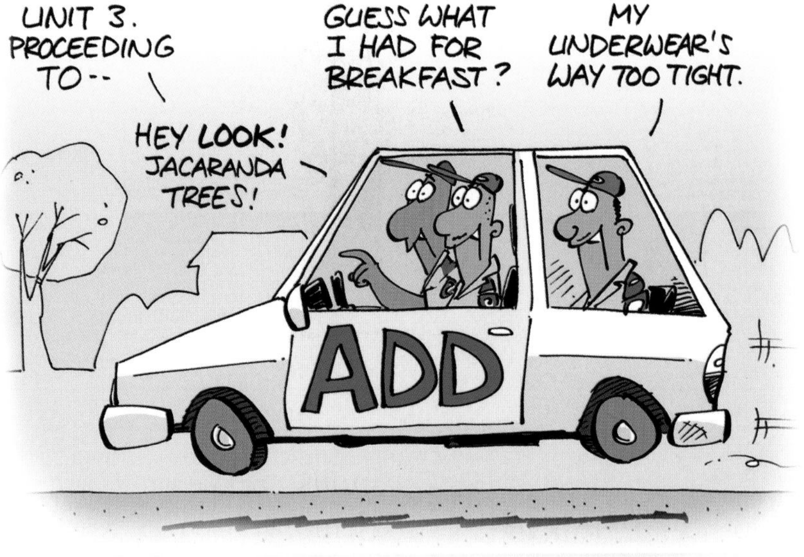
UNIT 3. PROCEEDING TO--
HEY LOOK! JACARANDA TREES!
GUESS WHAT I HAD FOR BREAKFAST?
MY UNDERWEAR'S WAY TOO TIGHT.
ADD

If your maid has an iron deficiency…
buy her a new one.

EVE SAYS SHE'S SUFFERING FROM AN **IRON** DEFICIENCY.
NEWS

IMPOSSIBLE. I JUST BOUGHT HER A NEW ONE LAST WEEK.
THAT'S WHAT I THOUGHT.

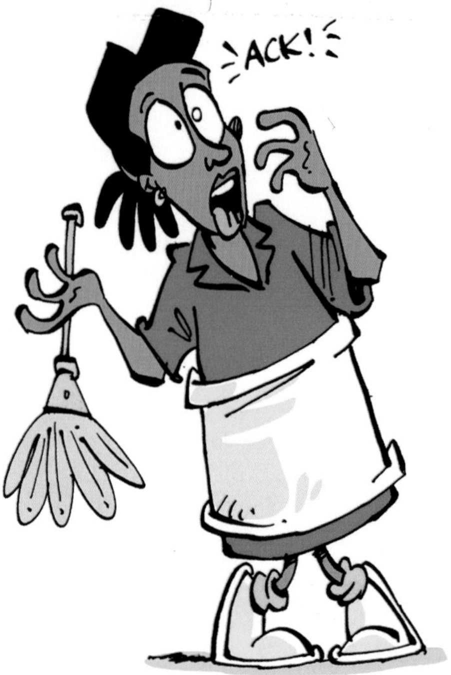
ACK!

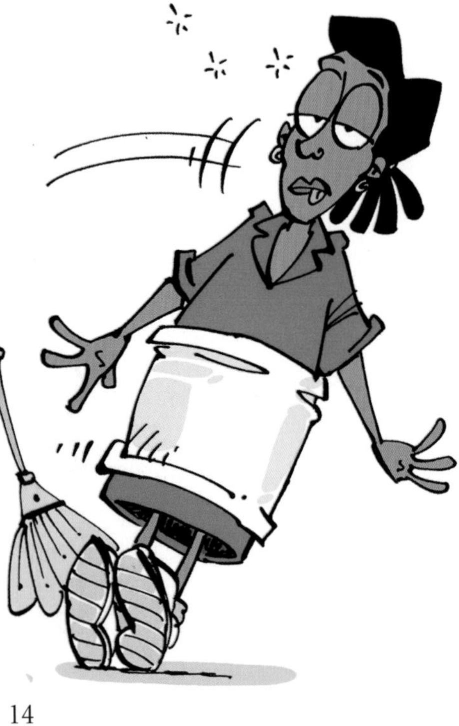

Hard work never did anyone any harm.

Never buy a 'previously-owned vuvuzela'.

Hope for the best… but expect Eskom.

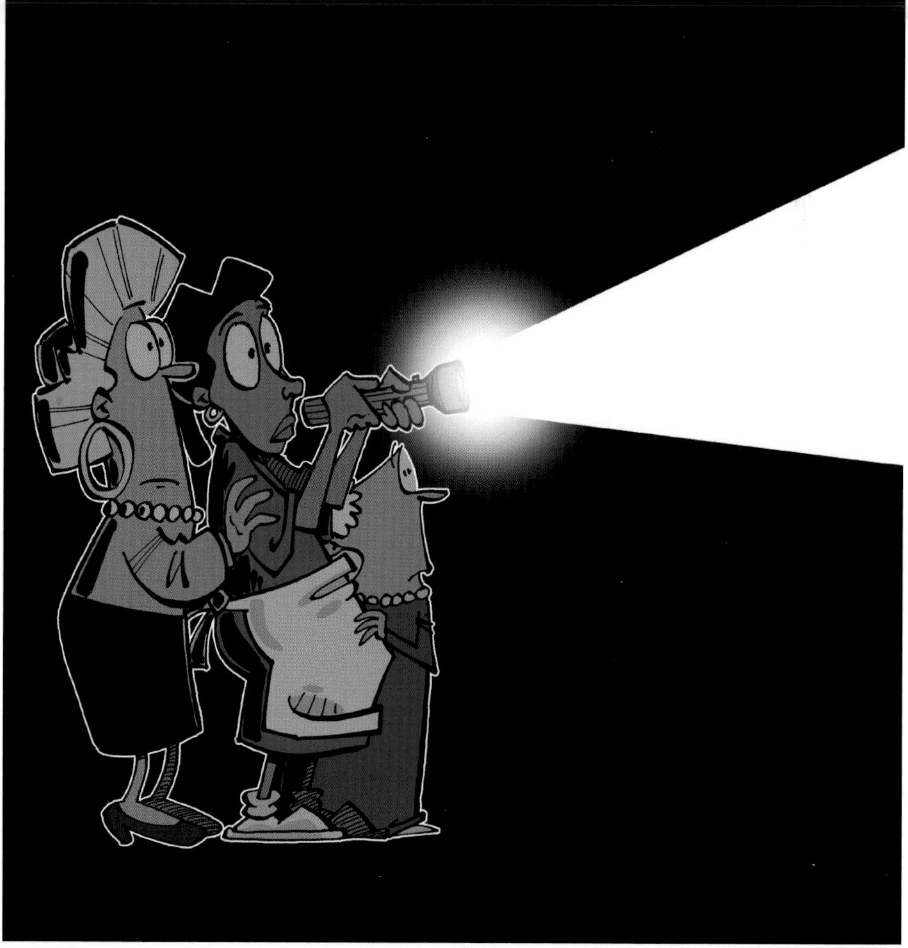

A katty saved is a katty earned.

I SHOT MY KATTY IN THE AIR.
PTING
WHERE IT LANDED I KNOW NOT WHERE.

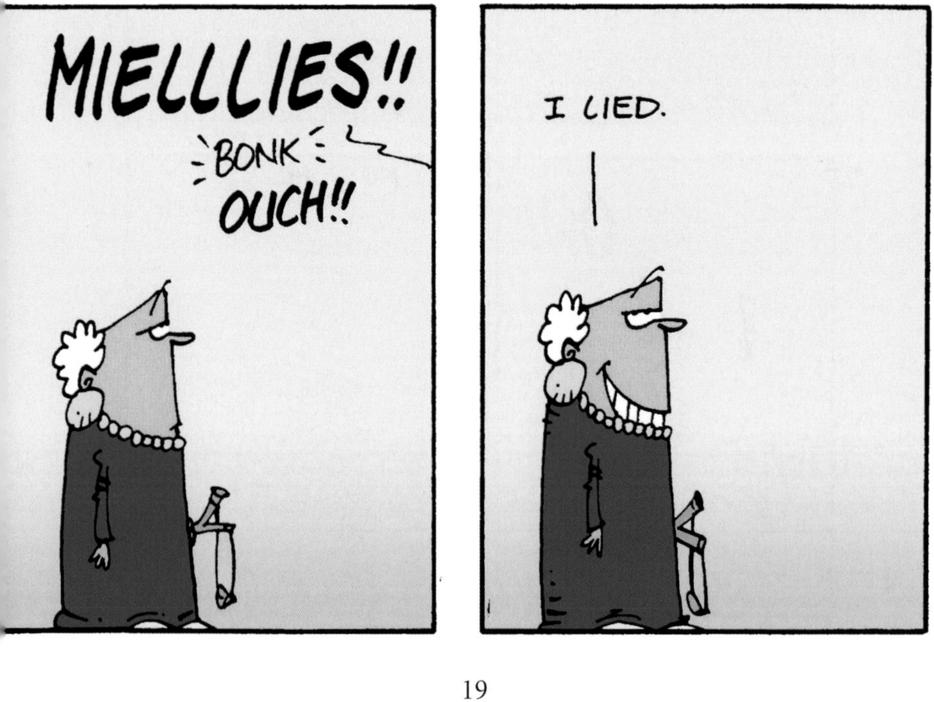
MIELLLIES!!
BONK
OUCH!!
I LIED.

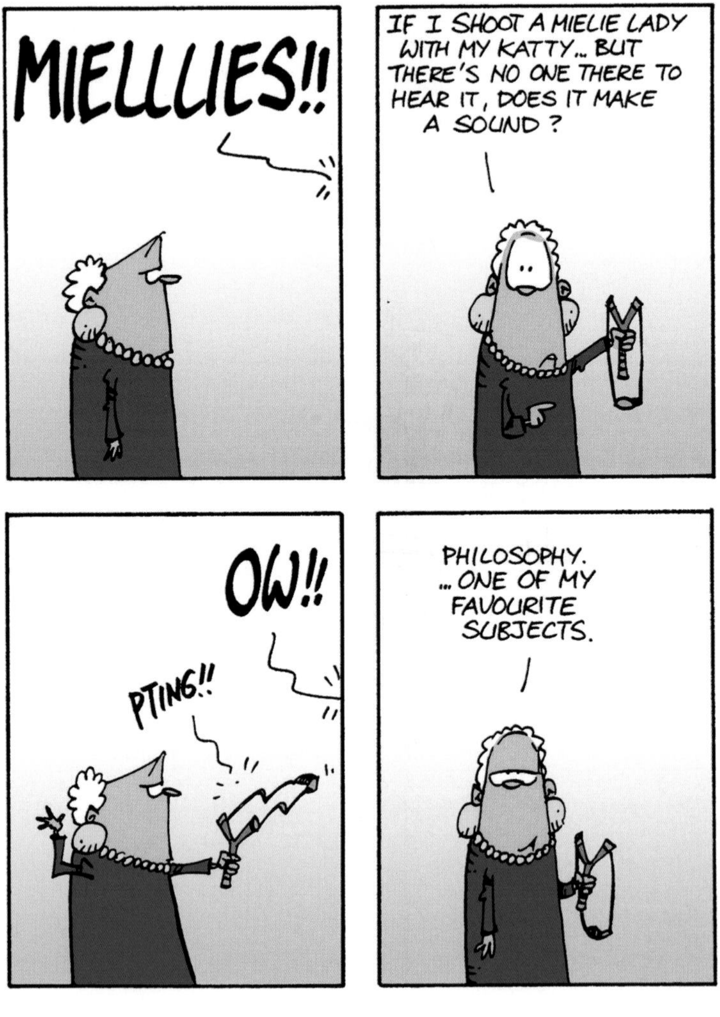
MIELLLIES!!
IF I SHOOT A MIELIE LADY WITH MY KATTY... BUT THERE'S NO ONE THERE TO HEAR IT, DOES IT MAKE A SOUND?
OW!!
PTING!!
PHILOSOPHY. ...ONE OF MY FAVOURITE SUBJECTS.

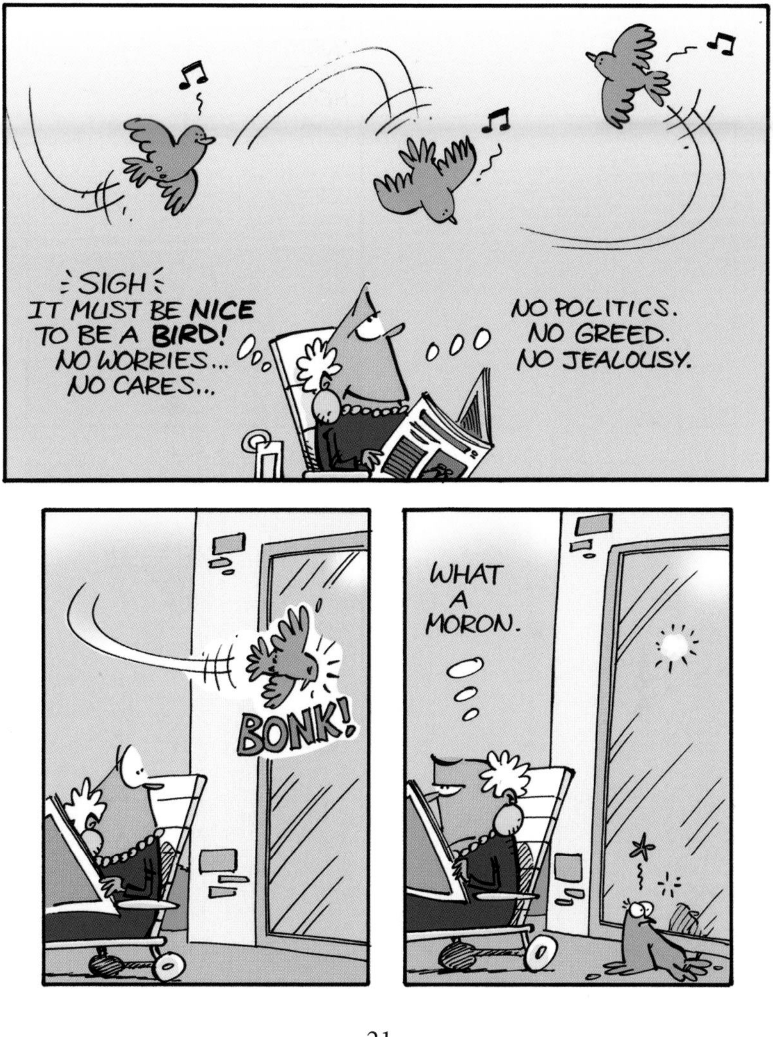
SIGH
IT MUST BE NICE TO BE A BIRD! NO WORRIES... NO CARES...
NO POLITICS. NO GREED. NO JEALOUSY.
BONK!
WHAT A MORON.

You're only young once...

TAP-ITY! TAP-ITY! TAPITY! TAP! TAP!
TAPITY-TAP!

... but you can be immature as much as you like.

LOOK AT THAT. WE'RE GONE ALMOST TWO HOURS...AND SHE STILL HASN'T MOVED A MUSCLE.

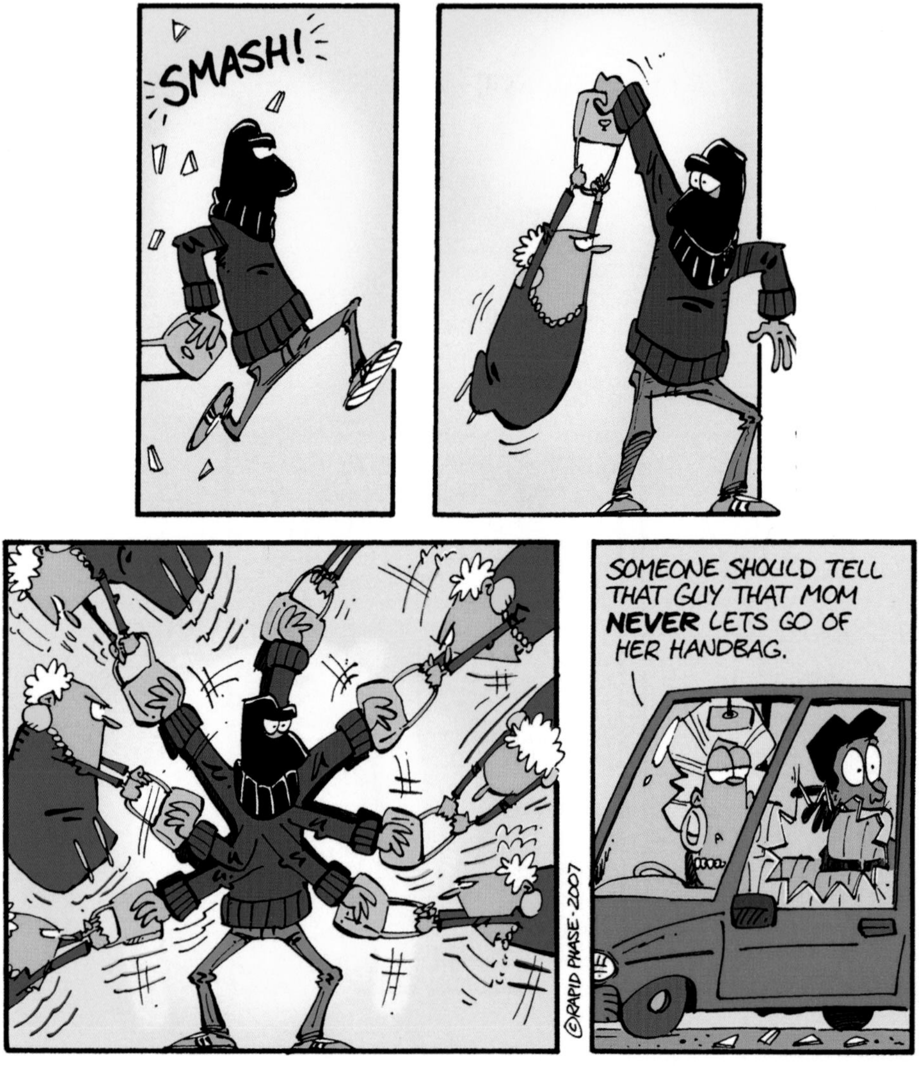
SMASH!
SOMEONE SHOULD TELL THAT GUY THAT MOM **NEVER** LETS GO OF HER HANDBAG.
©RAPID PHASE-2007

As you sow, so shall you reap.

... especially if the gardener doesn't pitch up for work.

Marriages are made in heaven.

But then so are thunder and lightning.

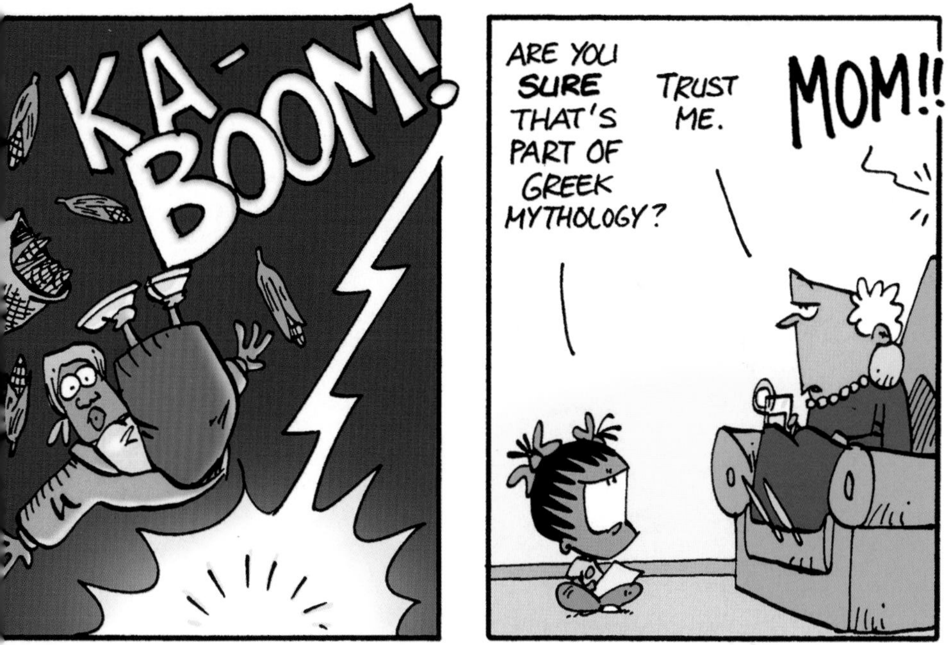
KA-BOOM!
ARE YOU SURE THAT'S PART OF GREEK MYTHOLOGY?
TRUST ME.
MOM!!

Change… is inevitable.
Unless you're standing in the queue to pay for parking at a suburban shopping mall.

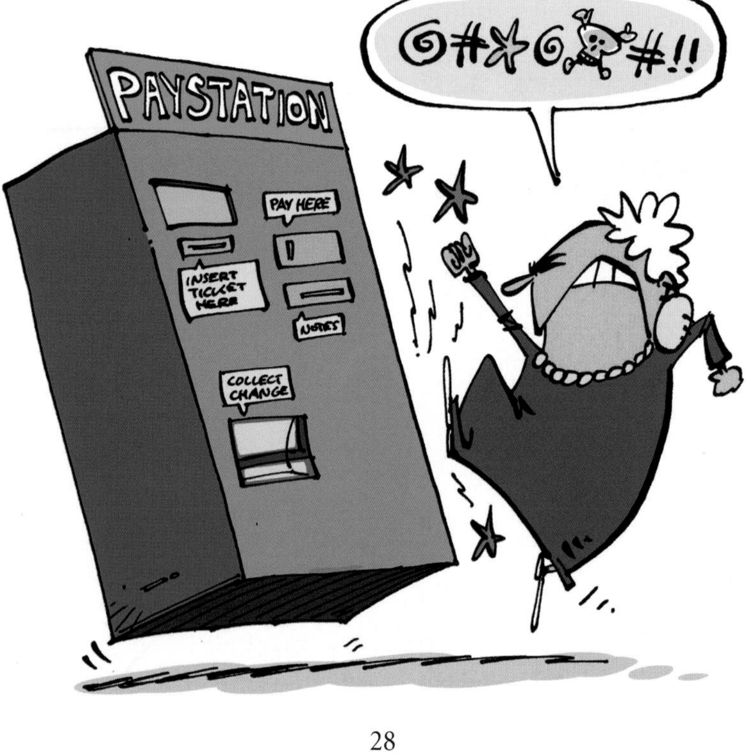
PAYSTATION
PAY HERE
INSERT TICKET HERE
NOTES
COLLECT CHANGE
#!!

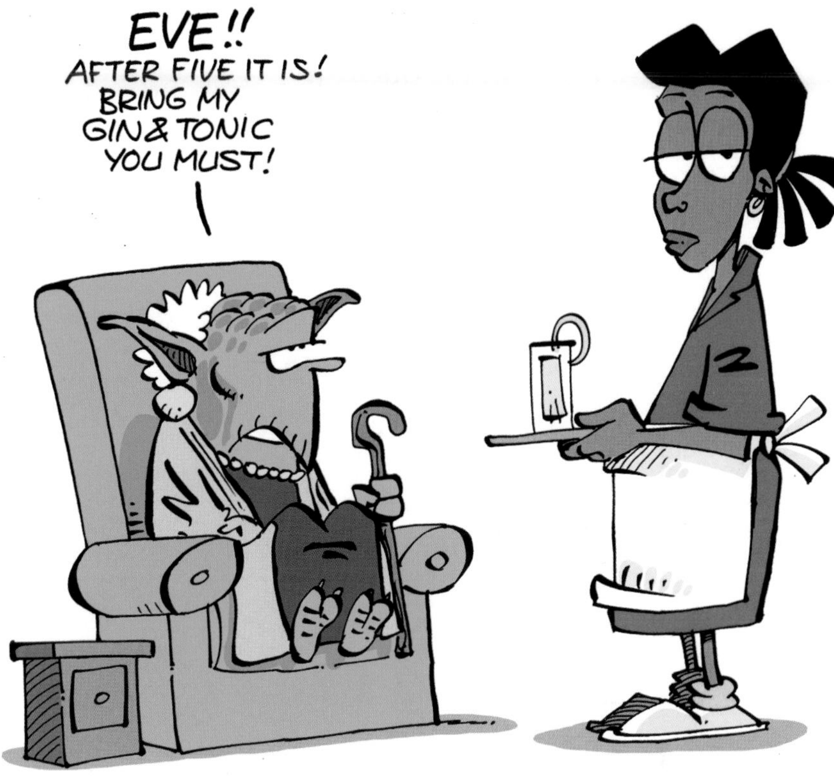
EVE!!
AFTER FIVE IT IS!
BRING MY
GIN & TONIC
YOU MUST!

If Yoda is such a Jedi Grand Master… how come he's never learned to speak English properly?

Laughter is the shock absorber that helps you negotiate potholes on the highway of life.

RING! RING!
EVE! IT'S AFTER FIVE! WHERE'S MY GIN & TONIC?!

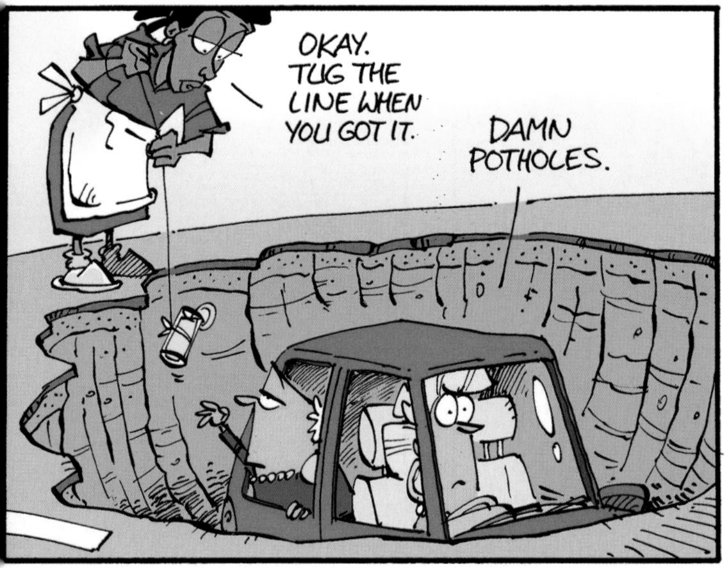
OKAY. TUG THE LINE WHEN YOU GOT IT.
DAMN POTHOLES.

The early bird gets the worm.

HARDEE DAH!!
THAT HADEDA SURE IS LOUD.
IT'S ALSO AN ENDANGERED SPECIES.
WHAT? HADEDAS AREN'T AN ENDANGERED SPECIES.

The early hadeda gets my katty.

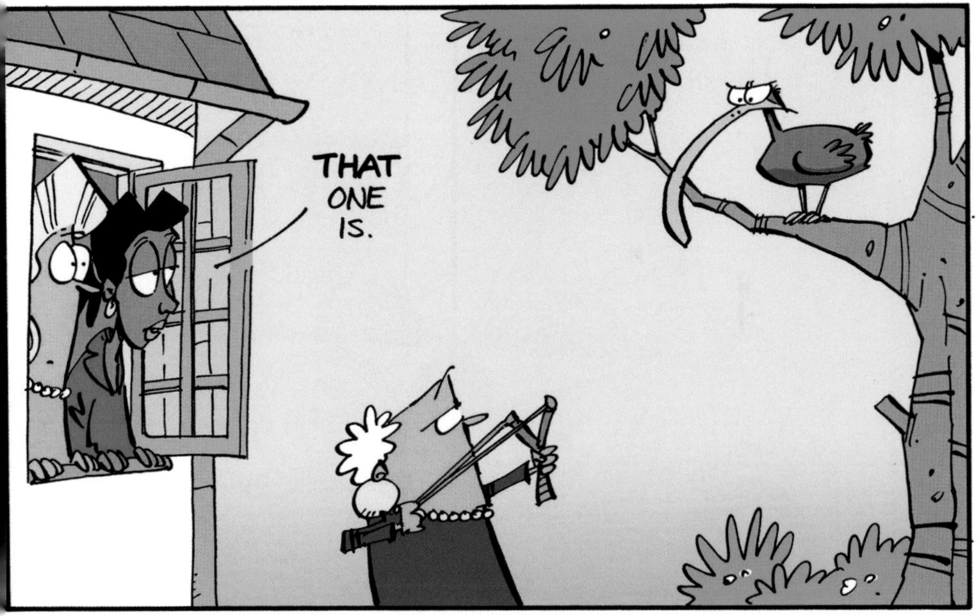
THAT ONE IS.

They say… that if you line up all the cars in the world end to end…

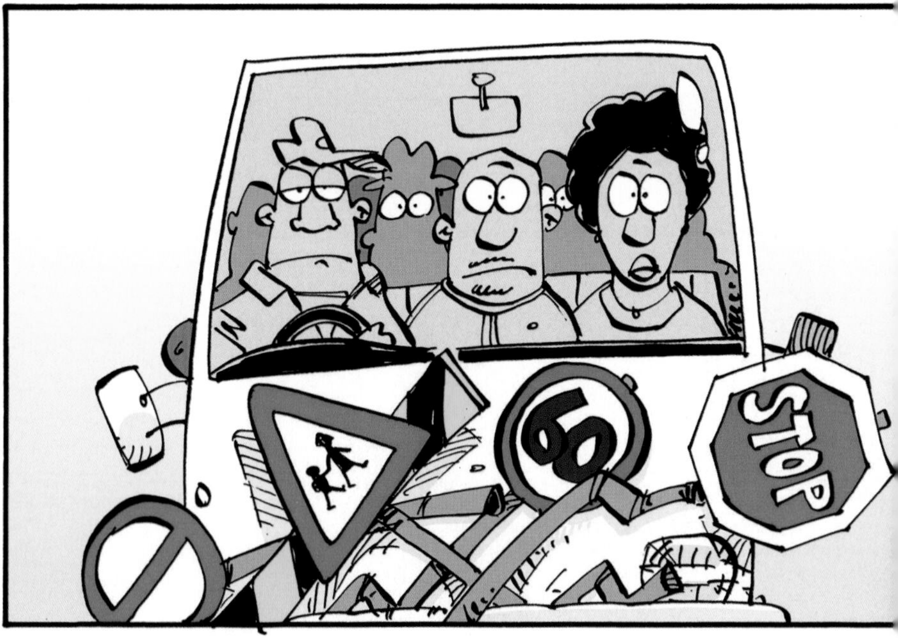
STOP
60

… some minibus taxi driver will
try to cut in front of them.

Make the best of every day…

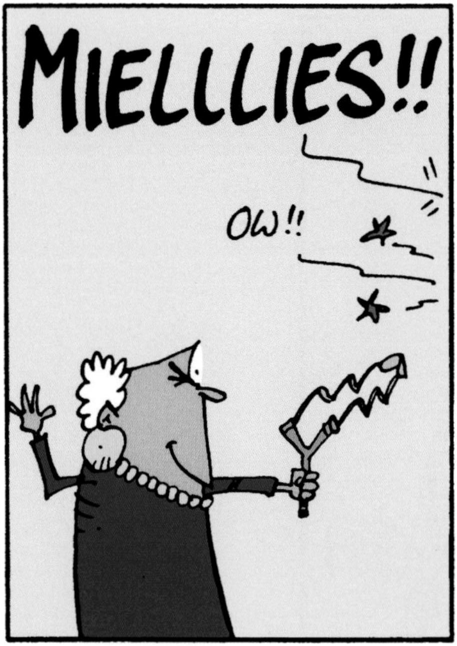
MIELLLIES!!
OW!!

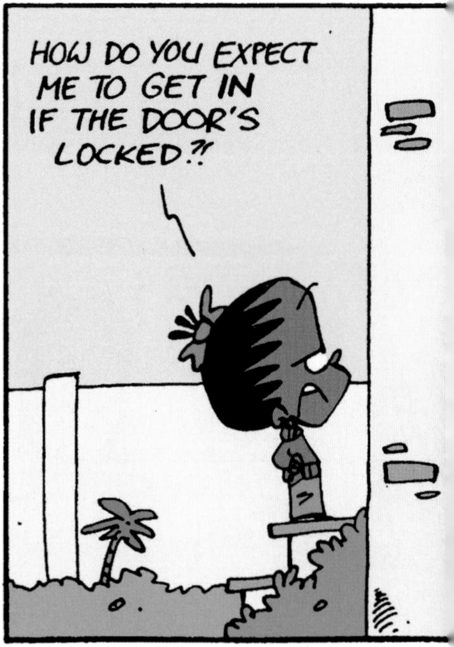
HOW DO YOU EXPECT ME TO GET IN IF THE DOOR'S LOCKED?!

… tomorrow could be even better.

OOPS.
TRIP!
SO FAR, I'M HAVING A GREAT DAY... AND IT ISN'T EVEN NOON YET.
CRASH!

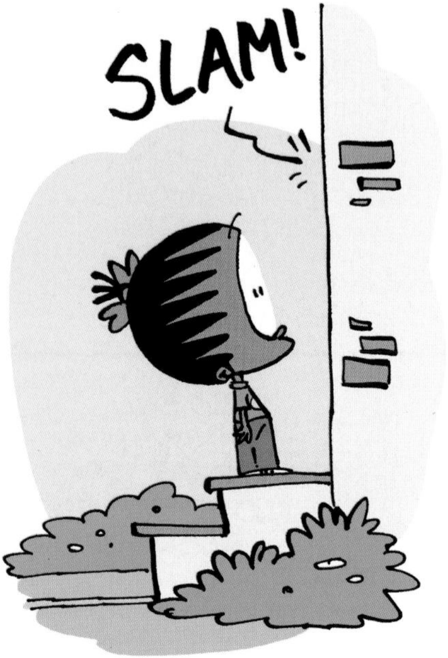
SLAM!

When one door of
happiness closes,
another door opens.

But often we look so
long at the closed door...

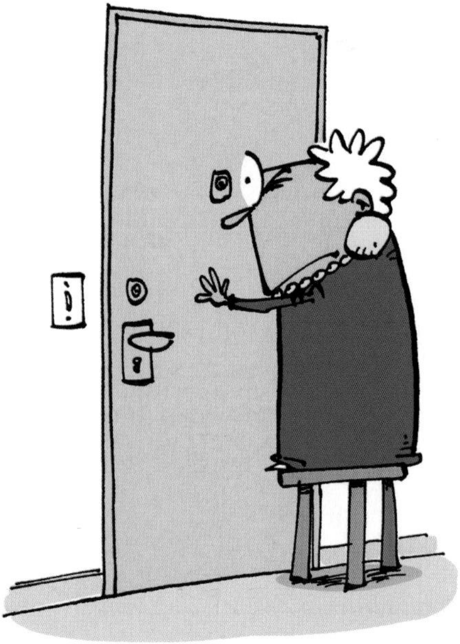

... that we do not see
the one...

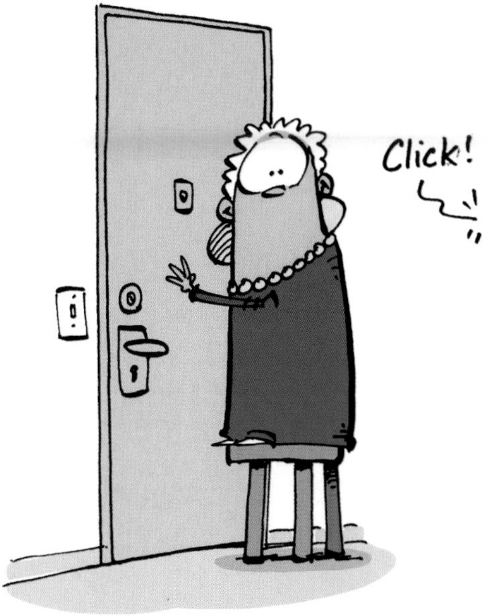
Click!

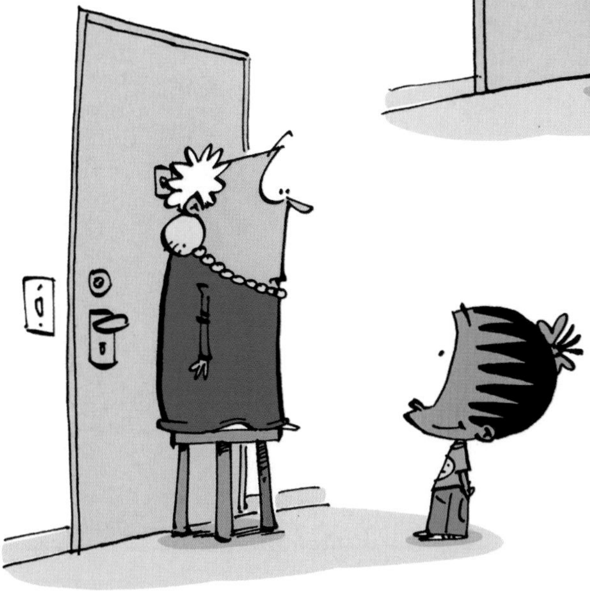

... that has been
opened for us.

Always take advantage of new technologies…

… because next thing you know,
they could be out of date.

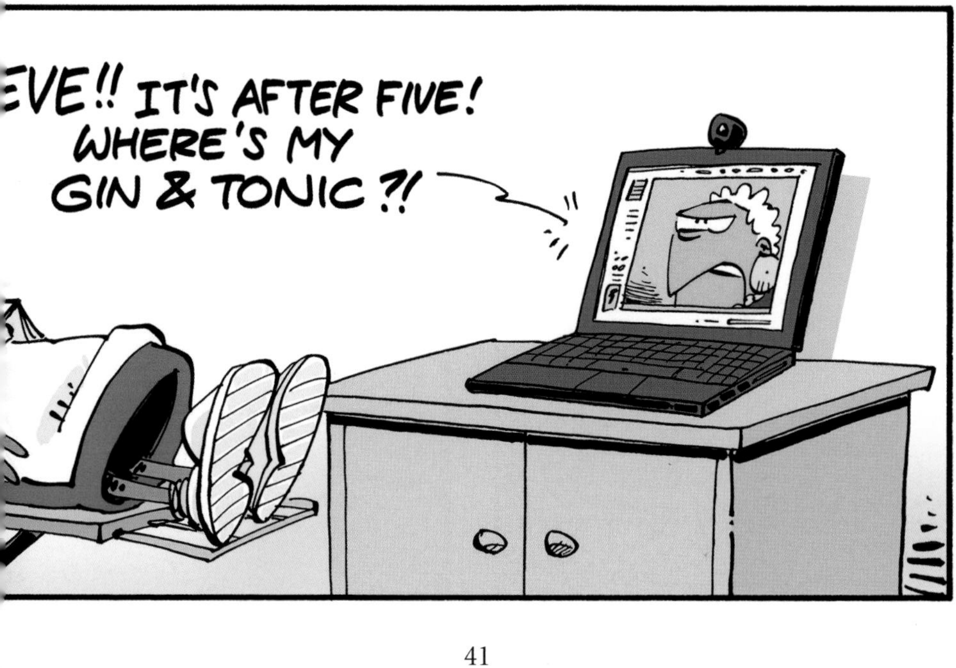
EVE!! IT'S AFTER FIVE!
WHERE'S MY
GIN & TONIC ?!

Always take time to smell the roses.

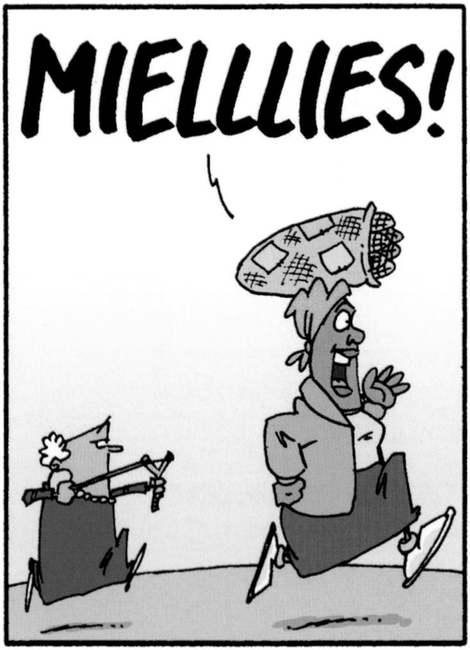
MIELLIES!

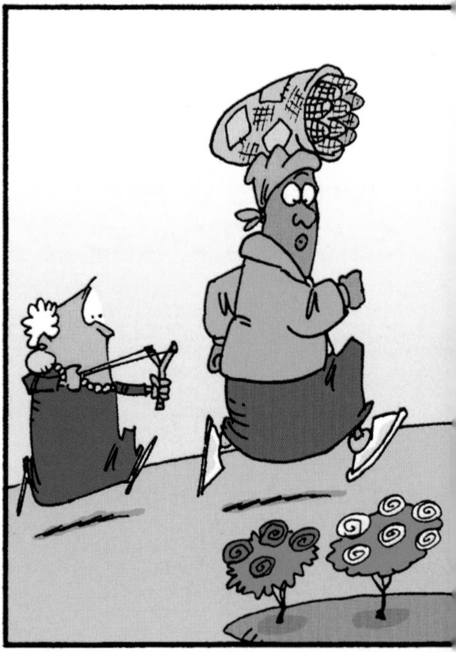

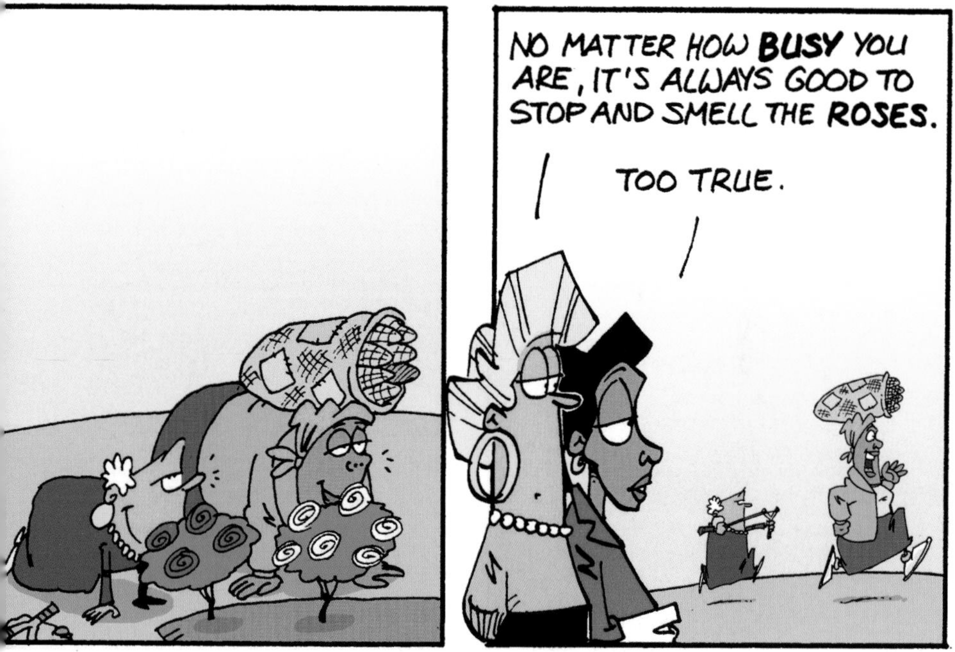
NO MATTER HOW BUSY YOU ARE, IT'S ALWAYS GOOD TO STOP AND SMELL THE ROSES.
TOO TRUE.

Carpe Diem.
Seize the day, then seize the ice cubes.

Plink! Plink! Plink!
Plink! Plink! Plink! Plink! Plink!
MOM! IT'S HAILING! DO SOMETHING!

To achieve the impossible dream...

SIGH
I JUST LOVE IT WHEN THE JACARANDAS ARE IN BLOOM... DON'T YOU, MOM?

... try going to sleep.

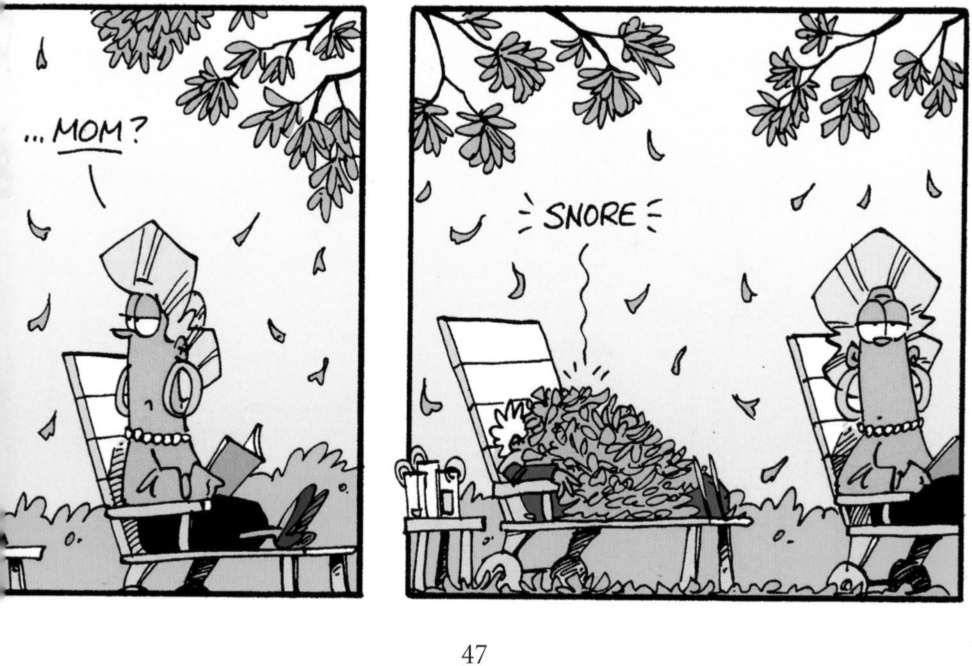

...MOM?
SNORE

Always maintain a healthy curiosity about the world around you...

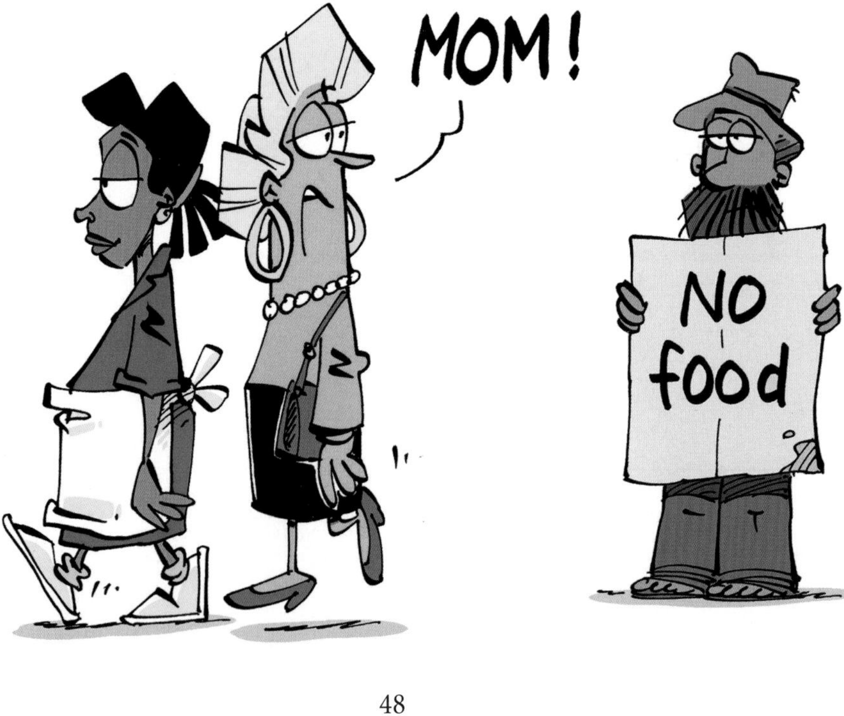
MOM!
NO food

... especially the things you just can't help but notice.

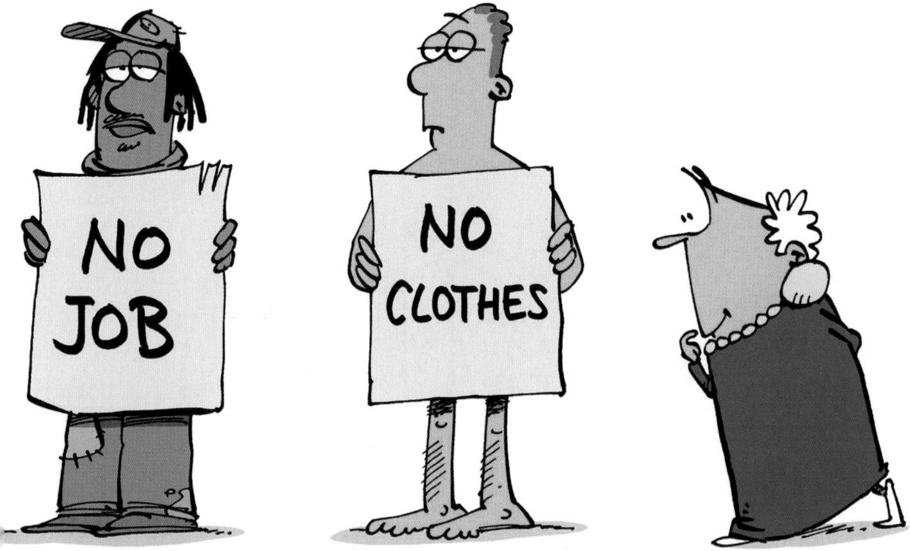
NO
JOB
NO
CLOTHES

If at first you don't succeed...

... destroy all evidence that you tried.

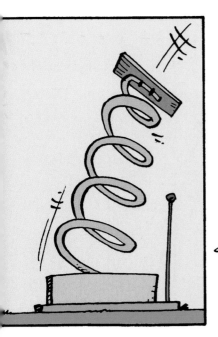

A positive attitude may not solve all
your problems...

... but it will annoy enough people to
make it worth the effort.

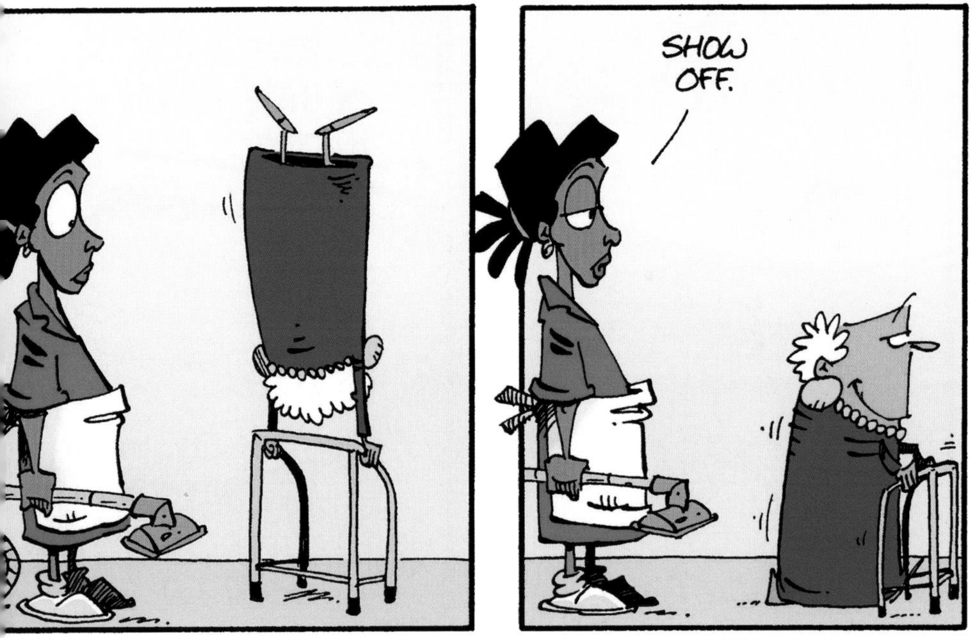
SHOW
OFF.

Roses are red
Violets are blue
Life is poetic
Just look around you

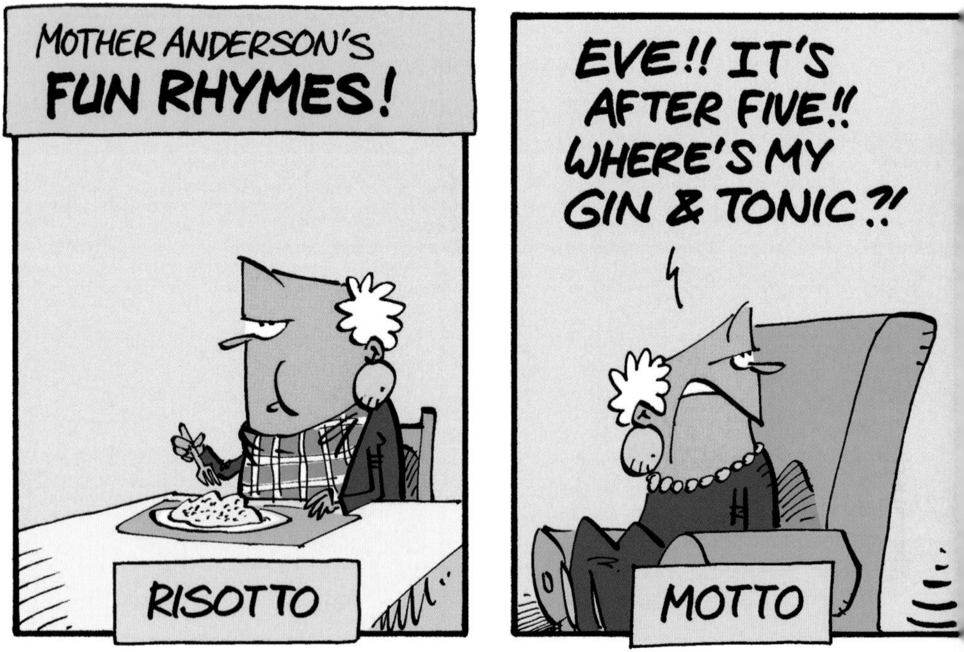
MOTHER ANDERSON'S
FUN RHYMES!
RISOTTO
EVE!! IT'S AFTER FIVE!! WHERE'S MY GIN & TONIC?!
MOTTO

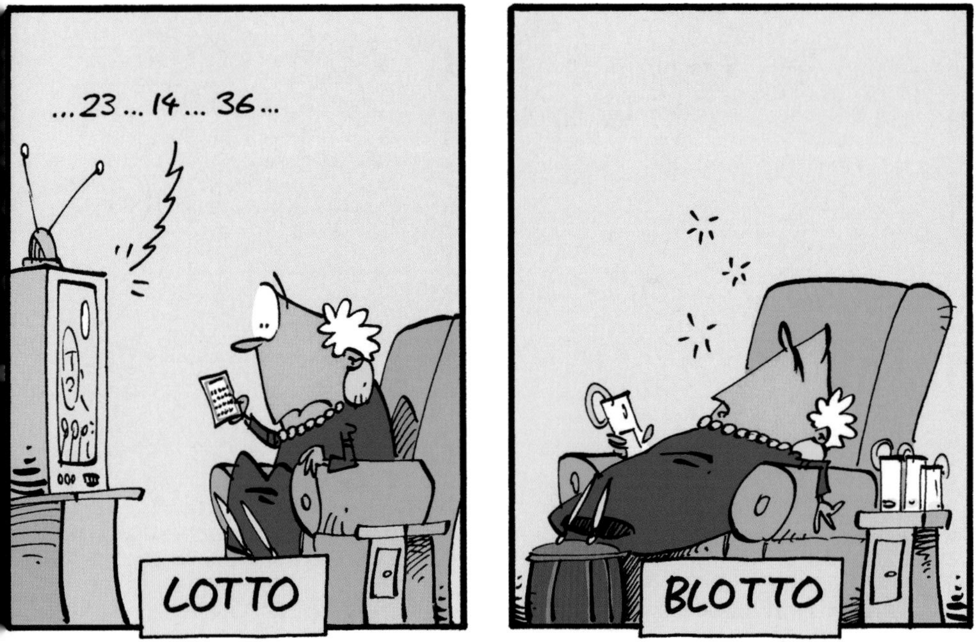
...23 ... 14 ... 36 ...
LOTTO
BLOTTO

Gather ye rosebuds while ye may,
Old time is still a-flying:
And this same flower that smiles today,
Tomorrow will be dying.

Especially if you buy them from some guy at a robot.

Roses are red
Violets are blue
Yesterday I gave
All my change to you

Roses are red
Carnations are pink
Don't forget
There's dishes in the sink

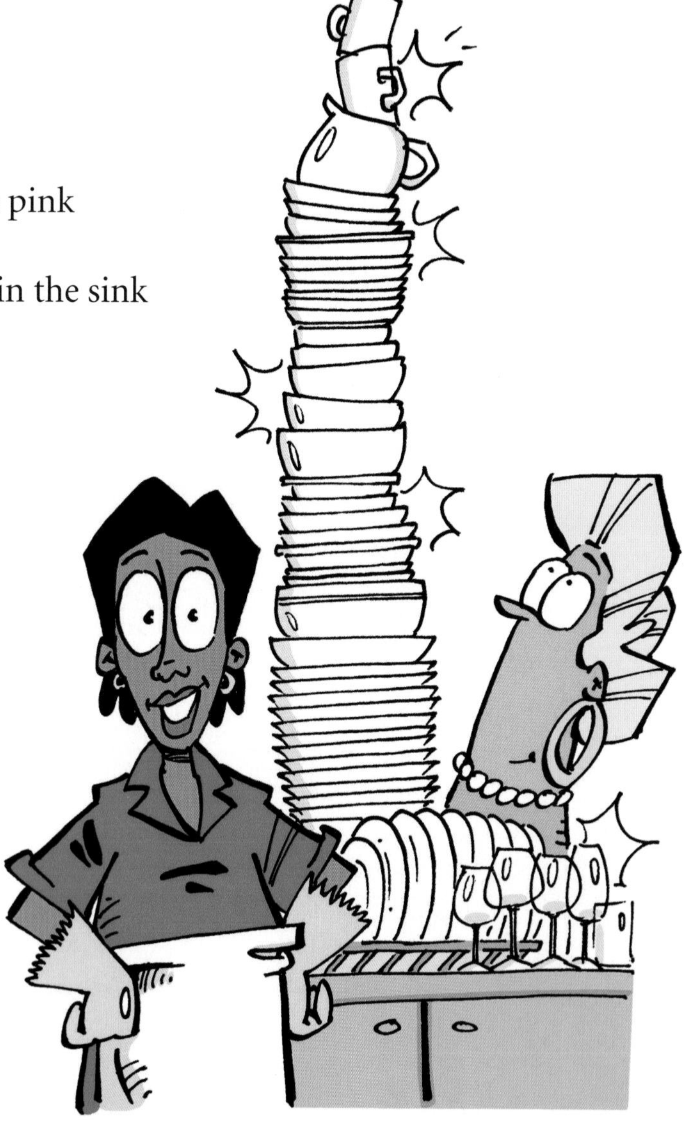

HEALTH & WELLBEING WISDOM

Having good health is simple. All you have to do is eat what you don't want, drink what you don't like, and do what you'd rather not.

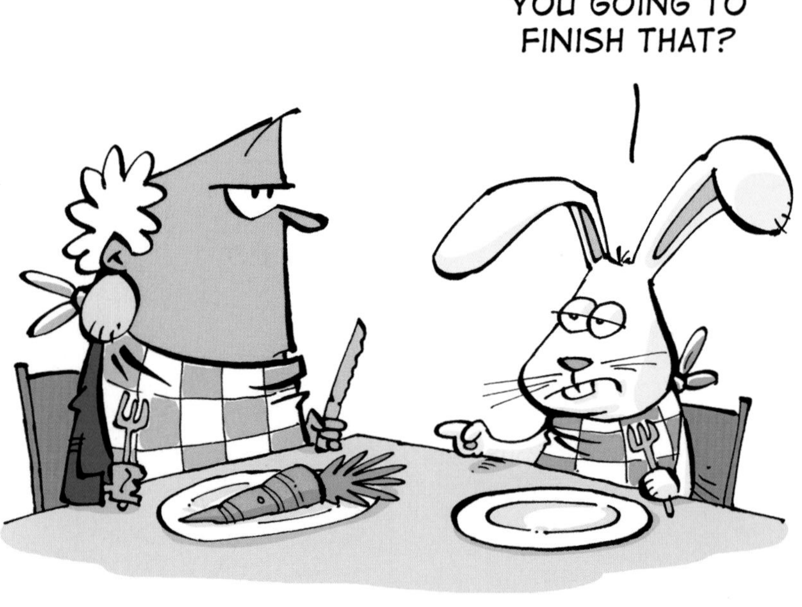
YOU GOING TO FINISH THAT?

Inside me is a thin
person struggling
to get out.

But I can always
sedate her with
two or three
gin & tonics.

SQUEAK
PUFF PUFF
CLANG!!
WHEW

SQUEAK
SQUEAK
SQUEAK
SQUEAK
SQUEAK
SQUEAK
SQUEAK
SQUEAK
SQUEAK
SQUEAK
SQUEAK

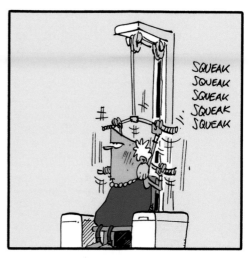

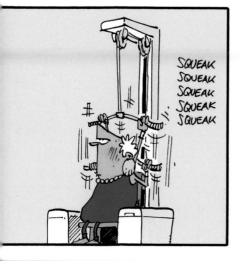

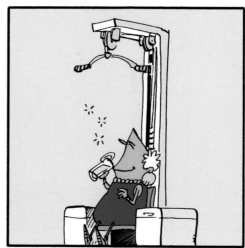

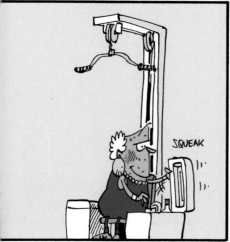

Exercise first thing in the morning...

... before your brain figures out what you're doing.

NICE TREADMILL WORKOUT, MOM. WHAT MOTIVATIONAL MUSIC ARE YOU LISTENING TO ON YOUR iPOD?
Puff! Puff!
Click
MIELLLIES!! MIELLLIES!!
Puff. Puff. Puff.

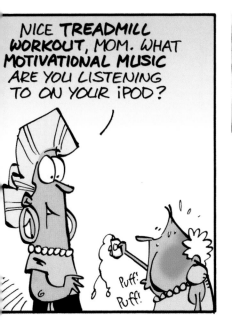

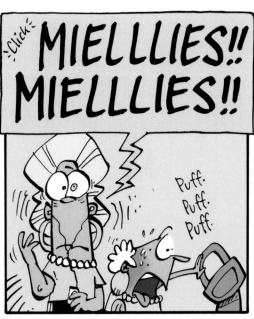

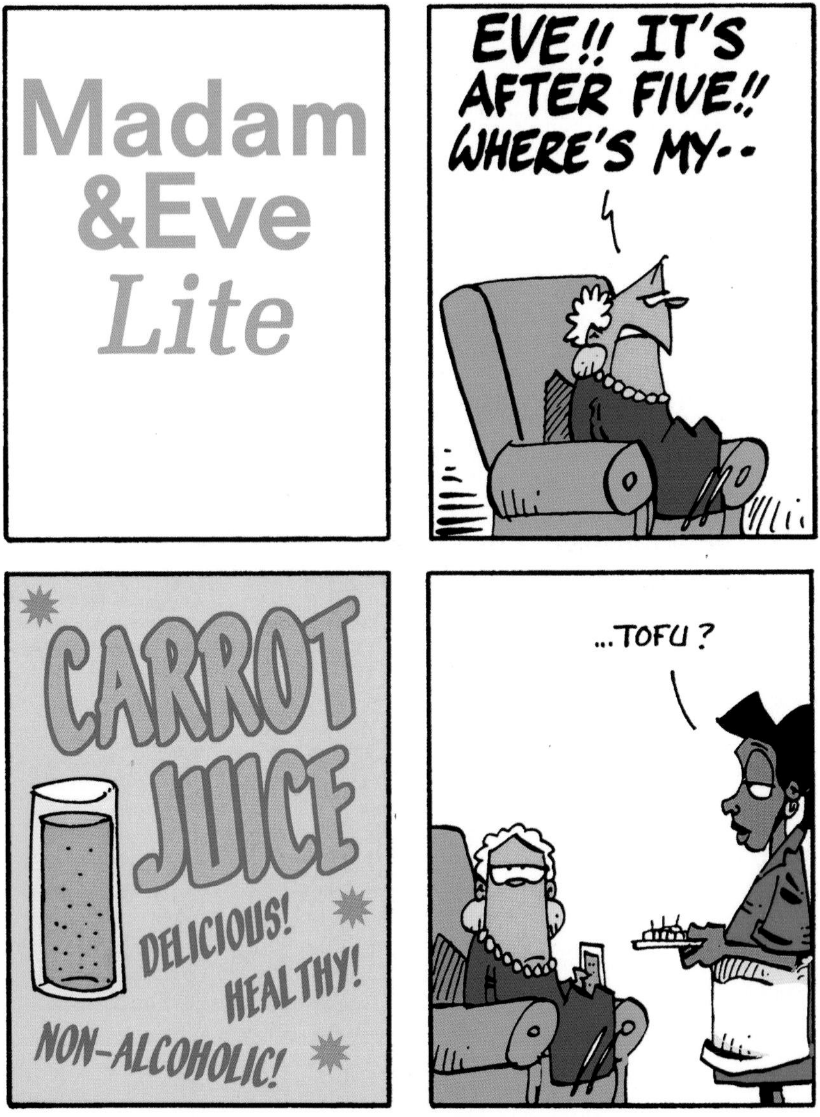
Madam
&Eve
Lite
EVE!! IT'S AFTER FIVE!! WHERE'S MY..
CARROT JUICE
DELICIOUS!
HEALTHY!
NON-ALCOHOLIC!
...TOFU?

More health and wellbeing wisdom

1. Take lots of naps. It's harder to get in trouble when you're asleep.

2. Early to bed and early to rise, makes a person healthy, wealthy and – sorry – what was I saying again?

3. All the things I like to do are either illegal, immoral or fattening. Luckily, the police accept bribes for the first two; the 'fattening' thing I'm still working on.

4. Avoid fruits and nuts. Stay away from any dinner where they eat food off of women… or any party hosted by Julius Malema.

The Heimlich Manoeuvre

THE HEIMLICH MANOEUVRE
WHEEZE
CHOKE!!
COUGH!!
PTOO!

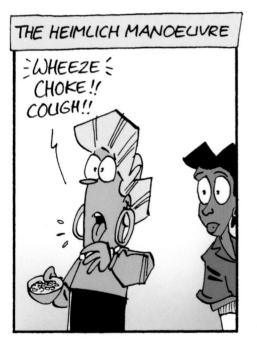

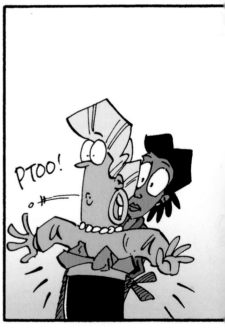

The Joburg Manoeuvre

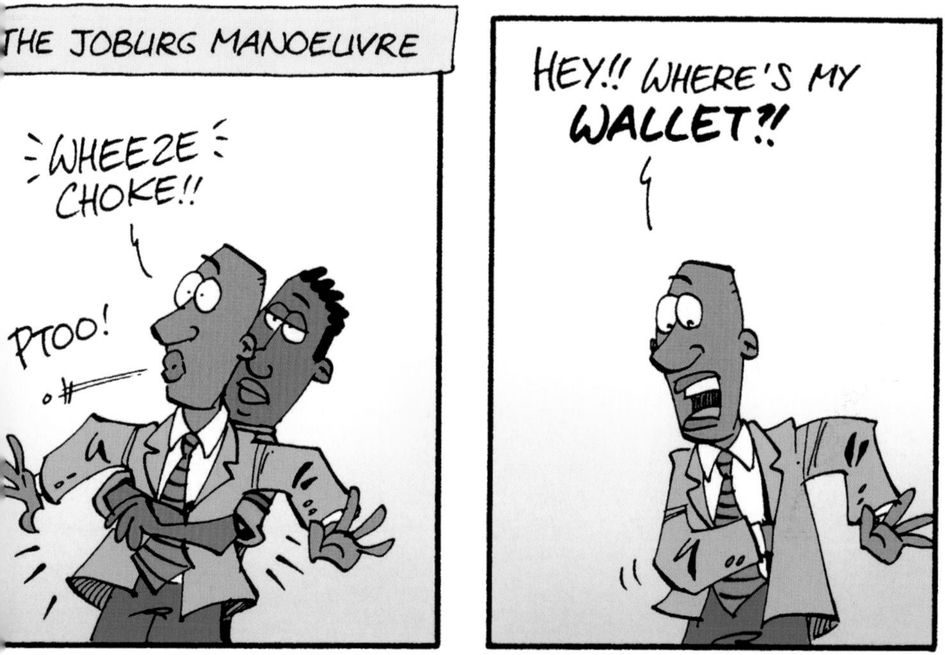
THE JOBURG MANOEUVRE
WHEEZE CHOKE!!
PTOO!
HEY!! WHERE'S MY WALLET?!

How to tell it's going to be 'one of those days'

1. The guy in the queue ahead of you is wearing a balaclava.

2. You shout 'strike' at a bowling alley and the staff down tools, and start toyi-toyiing.

3. The traffic cop finally follows you to an ATM to get bribe money… and there's a lit fuse attached to the keypad. (… and the screen reads: Twenty seconds until detonation.)

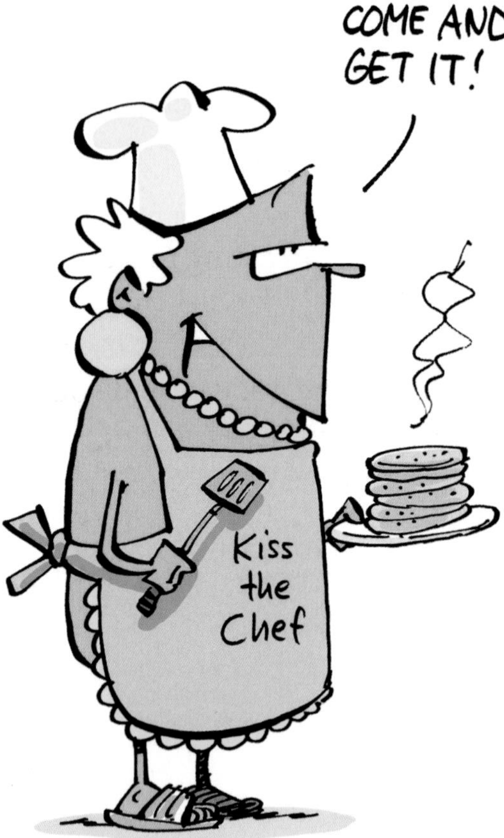
COME AND GET IT!
Kiss the Chef

Wisdom on 'cooking'

1. Always try to have your maid do it.

2. Never fry bacon while you're naked.

3. You are what you eat. So avoid eating moronic mussels, annoying salads, or jerk chicken.

4. When you return from a long holiday, and your maid's been on leave… open the refrigerator very carefully.

5. Always try to have your maid do it.

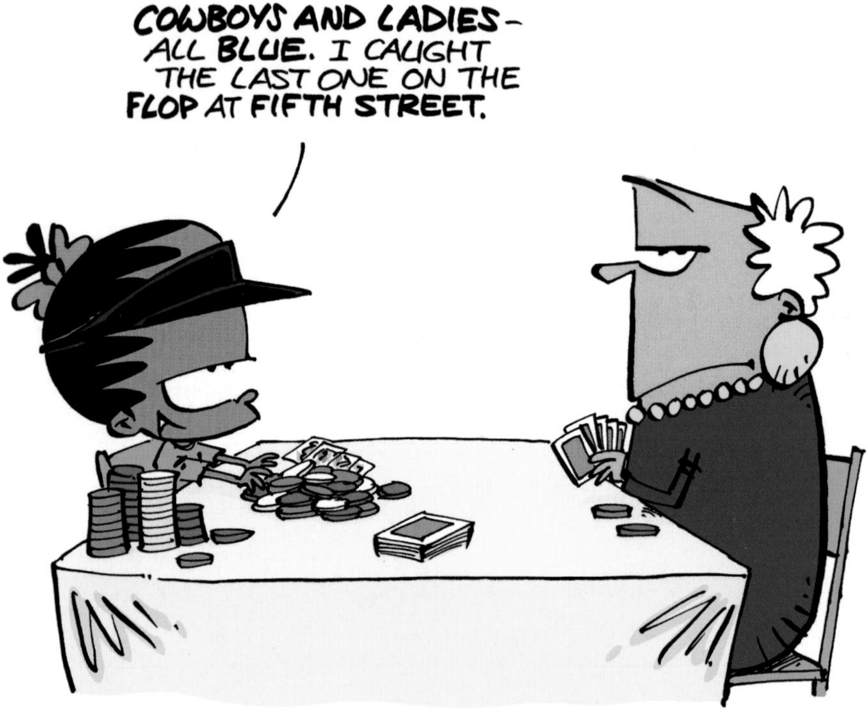
COWBOYS AND LADIES-
ALL BLUE. I CAUGHT
THE LAST ONE ON THE
FLOP AT FIFTH STREET.

Mother Anderson's wisdom regarding children

1. If your parents never had children… chances are, you won't either.

2. I take my neighbour's children everywhere. But somehow they always find their way back.

3. It's always fun to play board games with children. They're easy to beat and fun to cheat.

4. Watch out with poker, though. I've found that they pick that up rather quickly.

5. Anyone who says, "It's as easy as taking candy from a baby"… has probably never tried taking candy from a baby.

Everyone makes mistakes.
(The trick is to make them when nobody's looking.)

TO GET WHAT YOU WANT IN THIS LIFE, YOU NEED TO WORK HARD AND PAY YOUR DUES.
... DON'T EXPECT TO GET EVERYTHING **HANDED** TO YOU ON A **SILVER PLATTER**.

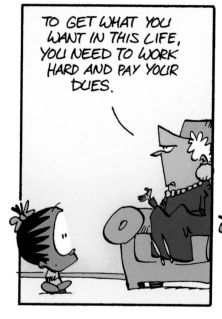

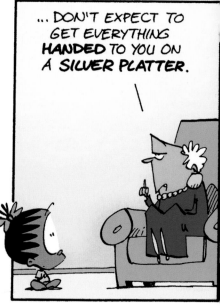

YOUR GIN & TONIC, MADAM.
WHAT?

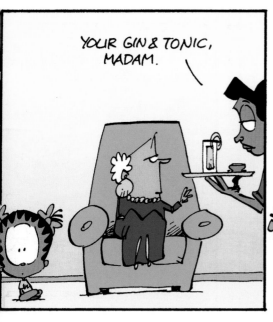

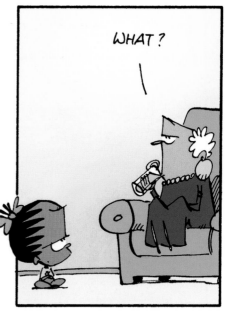

'The Seven Habits of Highly Effective Gogos'

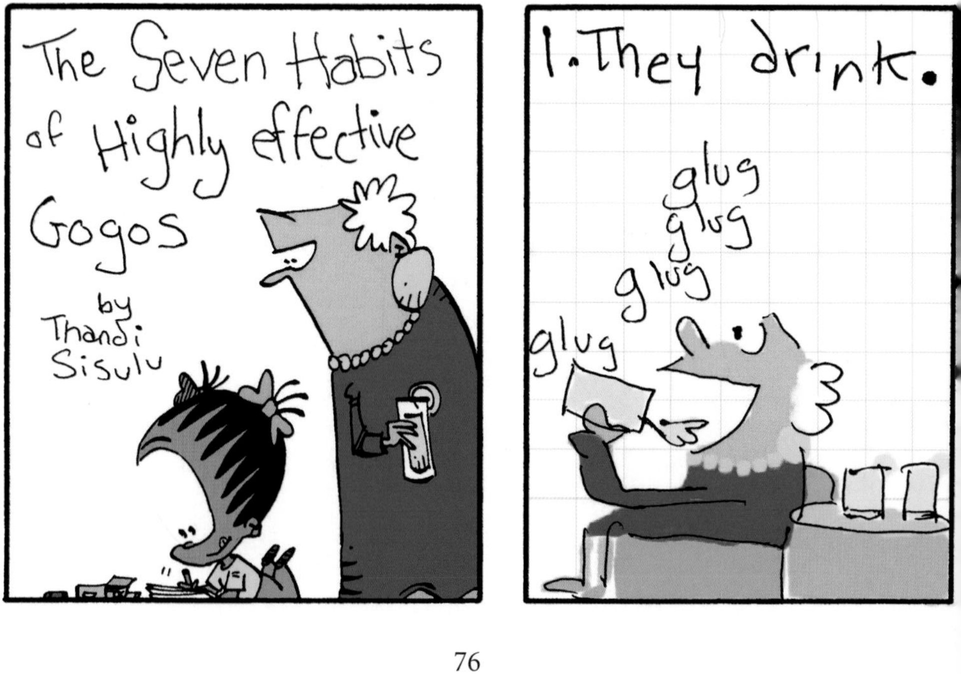
The Seven Habits of Highly effective Gogos
by Thandi Sisulu
1. They drink.
glug
glug
glug
glug

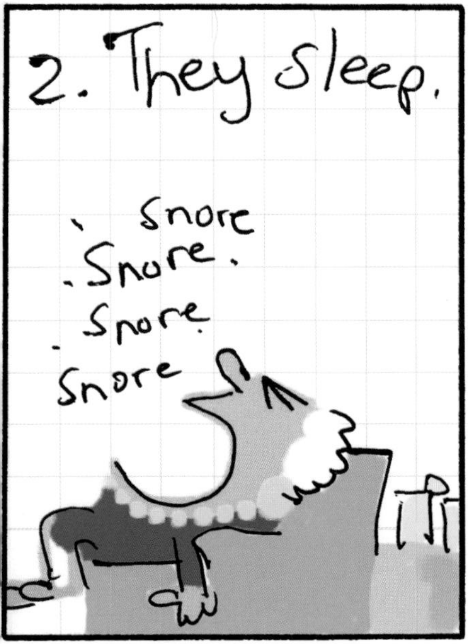
2. They sleep.
snore
Snore.
Snore
Snore

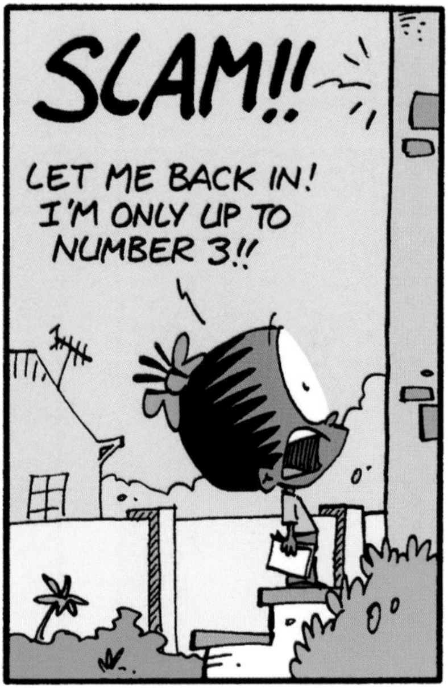
SLAM!!
LET ME BACK IN! I'M ONLY UP TO NUMBER 3!!

If you don't know much, try to know a little about a lot of things.

REMEMBER... SPACE... IS A GIANT VACUUM.

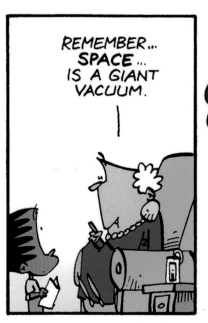

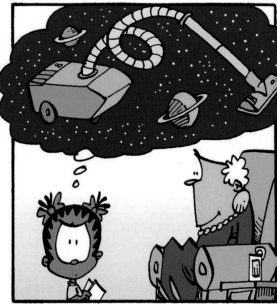

THAT'S THE LAST TIME I ASK YOU TO HELP ME WITH MY SCIENCE HOMEWORK!!

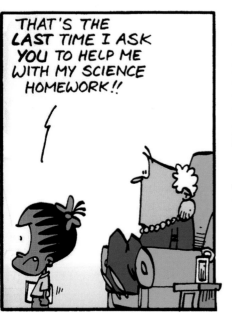

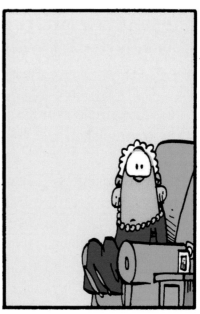

Driving wisdom

1. At a traffic circle, the expensive luxury car always has the right of way.

2. The expensive luxury cars with blue lights on the roof ALWAYS have the right of way ... or else!

3. If everything's coming your way... you're in the wrong lane.

4. He who hesitates... is usually the guy who arrives at the traffic circle at the same time you do.

5. Always take the road less-traveled.
   Less potholes.

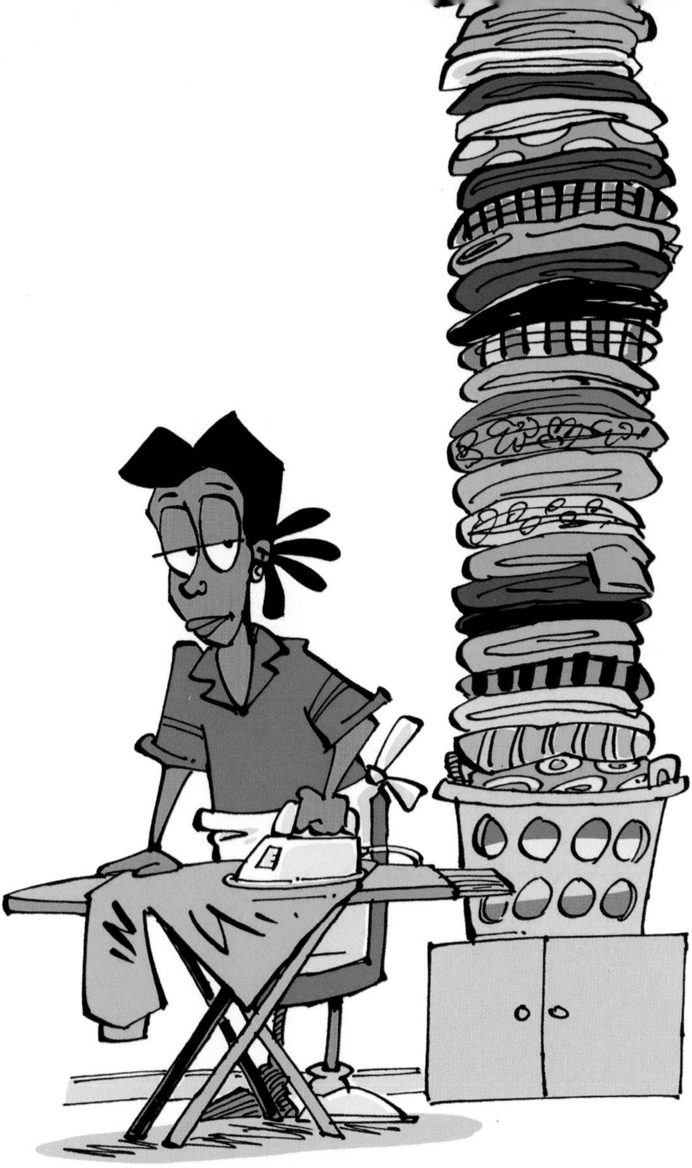

DOMESTIC WORKER WISDOM

How to tell if your domestic worker is lazy:

1. In the middle of sipping her tea, she pauses for a 'tea break.'

2. She wants the day off to attend Uncle Vusi's funeral. For the third time this month.

3. You can't teach someone to be lazy. Either they have it… or they don't.

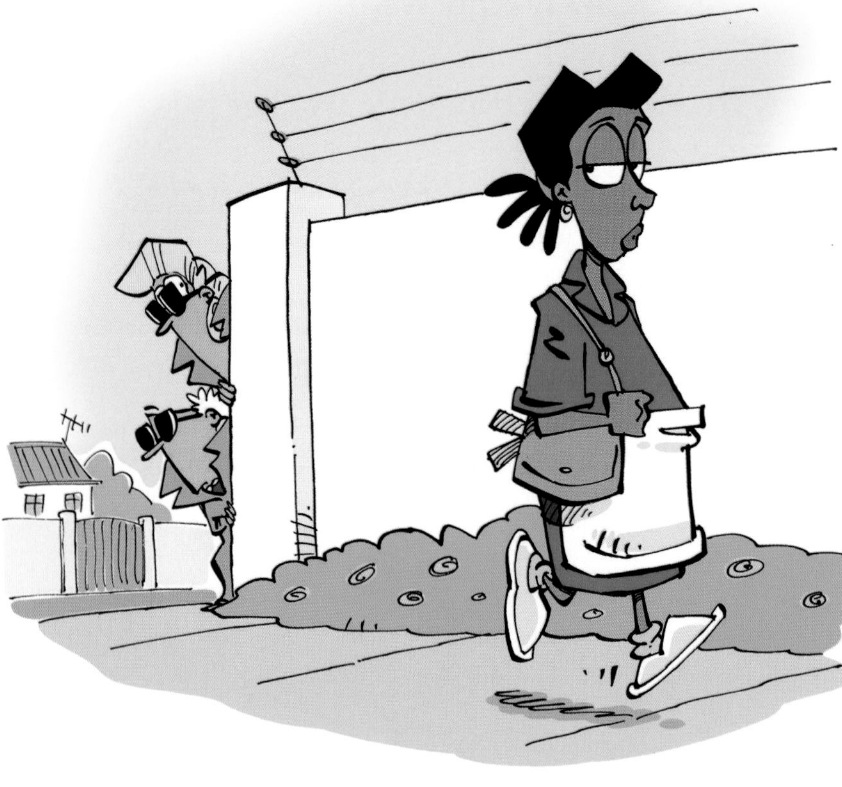

How to tell if your domestic worker is cheating on you – by working for another madam

1. She asks how much milk you want in your coffee … and you don't drink coffee.

2. She begins making sarcastic comments about the size of your vacuum cleaner.

3. You're sure she'd 'slip up' and shout out the wrong name – if only you both weren't called "Madam."

4. You notice she's wearing a new belt… and it isn't one of yours.

5. You overhear her tell the gardener she's exhausted from working a six day week. You already give her Saturday and Sunday off.

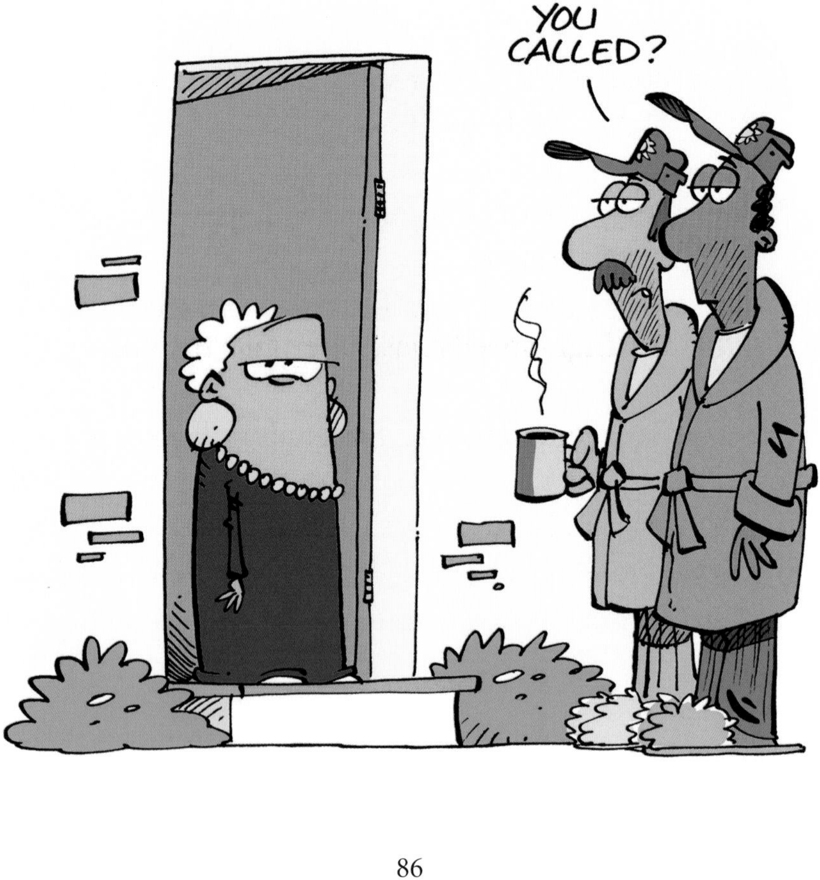
YOU CALLED?

How to tell if your local police are on a go-slow

1. They change their emergency phone number from 1023… to 1023-49867-378467-3854.

2. When they arrive on a call, they're still wearing their fuzzy slippers.

3. During a high-speed chase, they take the bus.

4. When stopping for KFC, they call for back-up.

5. When chasing a suspect, they yell: "Stop – or someone else will shoot!"

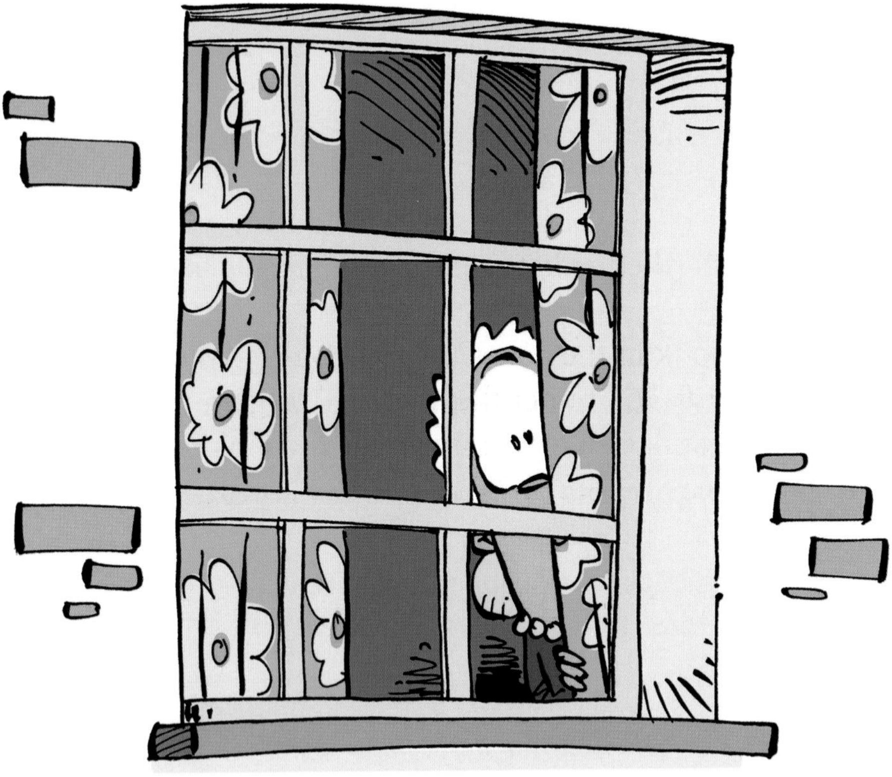

TOP 5 list of ways to tell if JULIUS MALEMA has recently moved next door to you

1. A long line of taxis queueing up the next morning with women passengers admitting they had a good time the night before!

2. … and they didn't even have to pay for breakfast!

3. You look in the new *Guinness Book of World Records*, and under the heading 'Largest Accumulation of Empty Single Malt Whiskey Bottles In A Single Location' … they list your neighbour's address.

4. The Sheriff of the Court seems to visit there a lot.

5. Why do you even need a list to tell you? Don't you already KNOW who he is??!

Mother Anderson's favourite South African musicals

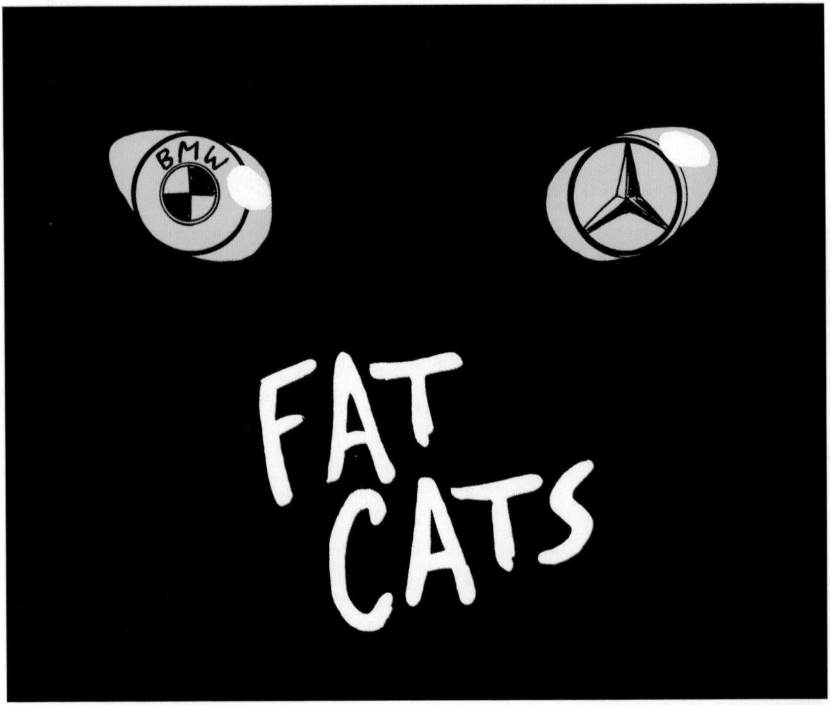
BMW
FAT
CATS

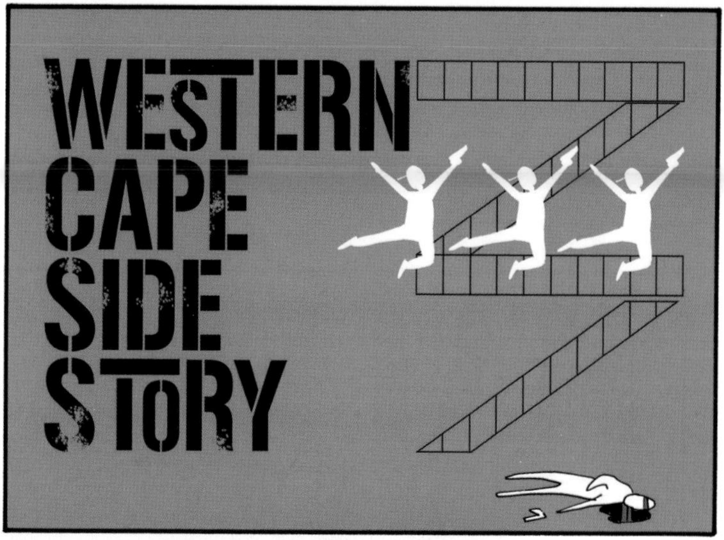
WESTERN
CAPE
SIDE
STORY

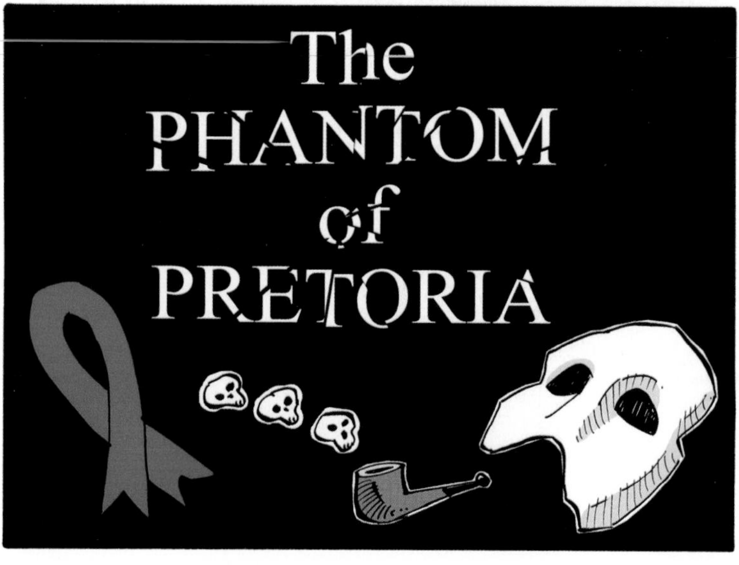
The
PHANTOM
of
PRETORIA

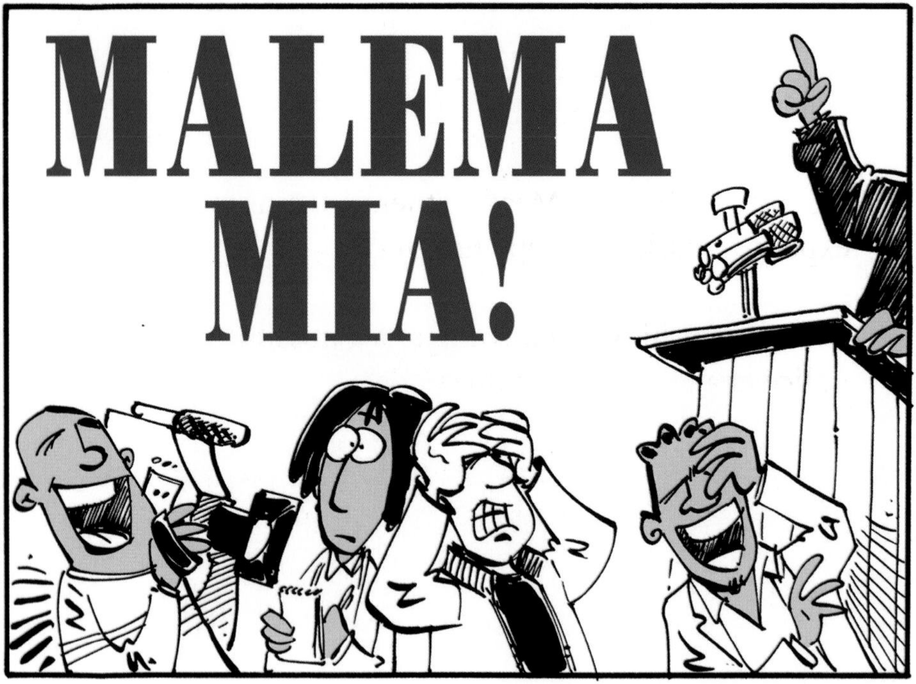
MALEMA
MIA!

'Suspicious accounting practises' that may indicate your local government official may be corrupt

1. He charges his wife's expensive tummy-tuck as a government expense, because they're running out of sushi tables for government parties.

2. Instead of a 'Happy Meal'… there are a number of expenses marked 'Happy Ending'.

3. Renting out his garden cottage as a possible new police headquarters for Bheki Cele.

4. Hiring an expensive new 'Bodyguard Contingent' with easy-to-remember code names such as: 'Uncle Vusi'… 'Aunt Florence'… and 'Father-In-Law'.

Mother Anderson's TOP TEN housework tips

1. Call Eve.
2. Call Eve.
3. Call Eve.
4. Call Eve
5. Call Eve.
6. Call Eve.
7. Call Eve.
8. Call Eve.
9. Call Eve.
10. Call Eve.

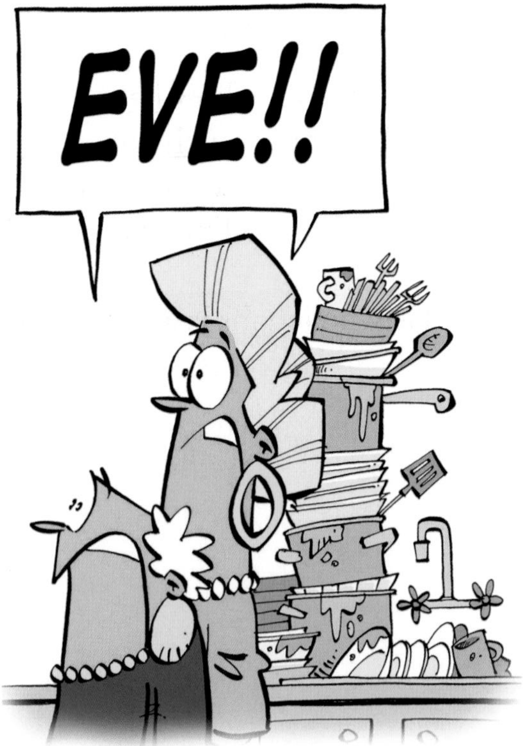
EVE!!

And think about it...

Always laugh when you can. Laughter is the cheapest medicine. Even so, I put in a claim to my medical aid… and they denied it.

Don't tell me how <u>hard</u> you work.
Tell me how <u>much</u> you get <u>done</u>.
And if I'm asleep, don't tell me anything.
Can't you see I'm trying to take a nap?!

He who laughs last… English is their second language.

A day without sunshine… is… well, night. Duh.

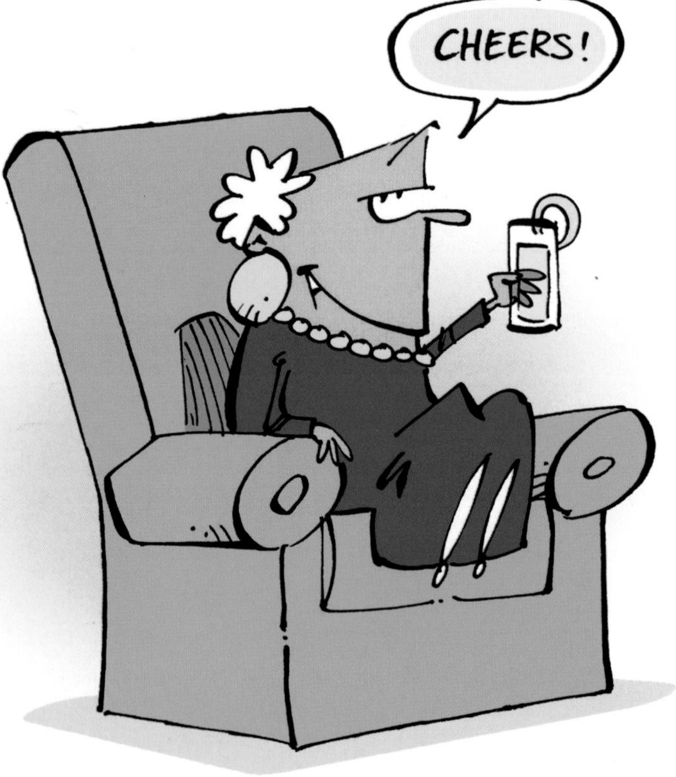
CHEERS!